THE
ALASKA
PURCHASE

by Daniel Cohen

Spotlight on American History
The Millbrook Press • Brookfield, Connecticut

Cover photograph courtesy of Alaska State Museum, Juneau,
(catalog number V-A-142)

Photographs courtesy of the National Archives: p. 10; North Wind
Picture Archives: pp. 14, 17; Alaska and Polar Regions Department,
University of Alaska Fairbanks: pp. 23 (Rare Books Collection Choris
#80083, Plate VII), 55 (Rufus Rose collection, #73-125-146N);
Library of Congress: pp. 25, 30, 45, 56; Alaska State Museum,
Juneau: p. 29 (catalog number V-A-50-4); University of Alaska
Museum, Fairbanks: p. 37; Old Dartmouth Historical Society-New
Bedford Whaling Museum: p. 43; Alaska State Museum, Juneau: p. 47
(catalog number V-A-142). Map by Joe LeMonnier.

Library of Congress Cataloging-in-Publication Data
Cohen, Daniel, 1936–
The Alaska Purchase / by Daniel Cohen.
p.   cm. — (Spotlight on American history)
Includes bibliographical references and index.
Summary: A close-up look at the events surrounding the
U.S. purchase of Alaska from the Russians. The author
shows the human foibles on both sides of what was later
to be regarded as a significant event in American history.
ISBN 1-56294-528-9 (lib. bdg.)
1. Alaska—Annexation to the United States—Juvenile literature.
2. Seward, William Henry, 1801–1872—Juvenile literature.
I. Title. II. Series.
F907.C63   1996   979.8'02—dc20   95-14180   CIP   AC

Contents

The
Alaska Purchase

Introduction

"Dark Deed Done in the Dead of Night"

The Alaska Purchase, the second-largest land deal in history (the Louisiana Purchase was the largest) was signed at four in the morning of March 30, 1867, after a hectic and chaotic meeting in the office of the U.S. secretary of state, William H. Seward. The Americans paid more than they had to. Russia would have been willing to accept $5 million for the territory. In his haste to close the deal Seward offered $7.2 million and the Russians snapped it up. Still it was an incredible deal: 586,400 square miles (1,518,800 square kilometers) of territory—twice the size of Texas—for a bit less than two cents an acre.

Later the artist Emanuel Leutze depicted the scene as a dignified gathering, with maps and globes and everyone looking very serious. The painting became famous, but it is inaccurate. There was nothing dignified about this deal. A critic called it a "dark deed done in the night."

The Russians had been in Alaska since the mid-eighteenth century. But mismanagement and a general lack of interest had led to a severe decline in the territory's profitability. By the mid-nineteenth century the government at St. Petersburg began to think of selling Alaska.

After suffering a shattering and expensive defeat in the Crimean War in 1856, the Russians actively began looking for a way to unload the land they felt they could not defend and could no longer afford. And the Russians needed money. There was only one possible buyer, the United States of America. Canada was still a British colony, and the British were not interested in expanding their North American territories.

Talks went on fitfully until 1860 when the American Civil War began and American officials became too distracted to think about Alaska. It wasn't until late 1866 that Edouard de Stoeckl, the Russian minister in Washington, was called home and instructed to get serious about negotiating with the Americans. He was told not to accept less than $5 million for Alaska. Stoeckl returned to Washington in early March 1867 and began bargaining with Secretary of State Seward.

To the Russian minister's surprise, Seward's opening offer was $5 million and when he hesitated, Seward upped the bid by half a million. The Russian was delighted. He used the new transatlantic cable to contact his government at St. Petersburg to say that he was going to try for six or even six and a half million.

Seward had already been given the authority by President Andrew Johnson and his Cabinet to pay as much as $7 million for the land. The approval was almost casual. No one in the government except Seward was much interested in Alaska.

By March 23, most of the details of the sale had been worked out. Stoeckl had managed to get the price up to the full $7 million. He cabled St. Petersburg for authority to sign a treaty. The Russian minister was almost embarrassed by the speed and success of his negotiations. It had taken only two weeks. Said Stoeckl: "This whole affair has been managed in the go-ahead way of the Americans."

Approval came from St. Petersburg on March 29, and that evening the Russian dropped by Seward's home to give him the good news. He told the secretary of state that he would come by the State Department on the following day to work out the final details.

Seward's reply was pure "go-ahead" American: "Why wait until tomorrow, Mr. Stoeckl? Let us make the treaty tonight."

The Russian was surprised and a bit suspicious. He said the Department of State was already closed and that all the clerks and secretaries had gone home.

Seward waved aside the objection. He said that if the Russian would bring his assistants together and come to the State Department before midnight he would find it open and ready for business.

Seward rounded up his secretaries and clerks and sent his son to get Massachusetts Senator Charles Sumner. Congress would have to approve any treaty, and Seward knew that Sumner, the powerful chairman of the committee on foreign affairs, was the key to such approval. Sumner was less than enthusiastic about the hasty deal. He did not even attend the signing ceremony, though Leutze put him in the official picture anyway.

Stoeckl wanted to change a few minor points in the treaty, but Seward didn't want any delays or complications at this point. He tacked on another $200,000 to the price to quiet any Russian objections.

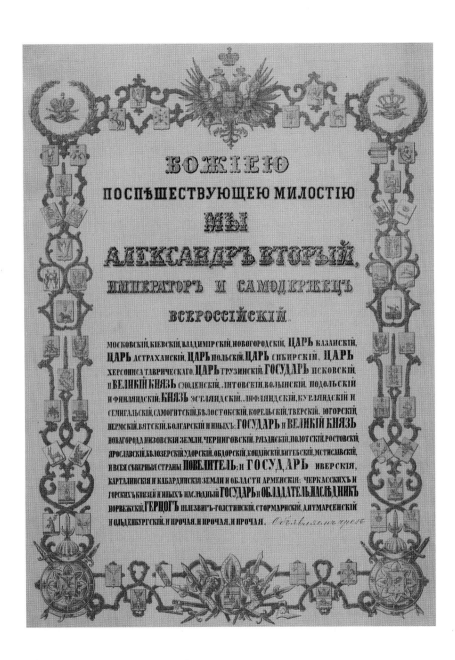

By 4 A.M. two copies of the treaty had been prepared. The treaty was a mere twenty-seven pages long. The copies were brought into Seward's gas-lighted office and officially signed.

A few years later a friend asked Seward what he considered the most significant act of his career. Without hesitation he replied, "The purchase of Alaska! But it will take the people a generation to find it out."

He was right on both counts, though it took more than a generation.

The Russian copy of the Alaska Purchase Treaty, which was signed at 4:00 A.M. on March 30, 1867.

1

The "Discovery" of Alaska

A laska was probably the first part of the North American continent that was "discovered" by human beings. Just exactly when this happened we do not know. But for many thousands of years Alaska and the part of Asia now called Siberia were connected. Then, somewhere around 10,000 years ago, sea levels changed. The land connection between Asia and North America was broken by what we now call the Bering Strait.

Though no one knows for certain, the prevailing theory is that before the connection was broken, wanderers from Asia walked across the land bridge and into North America. These Asian wanderers were the ancestors of the Native Americans. Native Alaskans include three general groups: Aleuts, Eskimos (or Inuit) and Tlingit and other Indians. Even after the land bridge was severed, Siberian and Alaskan natives regularly crossed the narrow Bering Strait to trade.

Aside from these contacts, it was ages before anyone from the outside world visited Alaska. There is no clear record of when Alaska was first visited by travelers from Europe, though it was probably sometime in the seventeenth century. The recorded his-

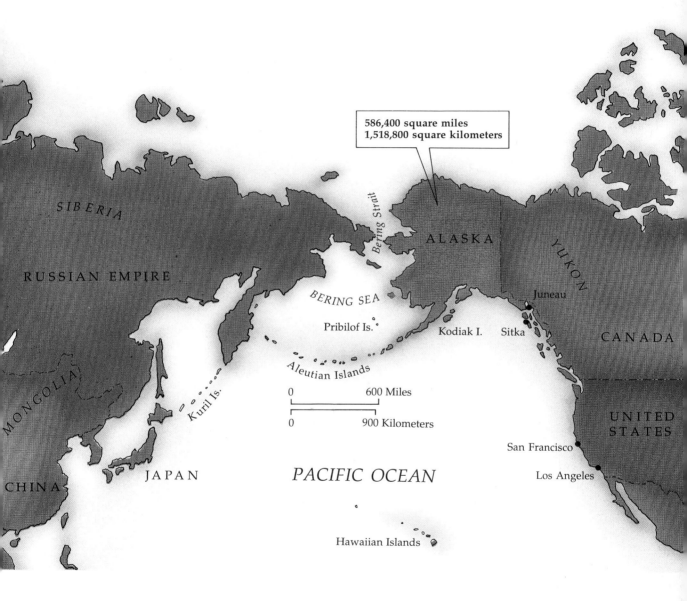

586,400 square miles
1,518,800 square kilometers

SIBERIA

RUSSIAN EMPIRE

Bering Strait

ALASKA

YUKON

BERING SEA

Pribilof Is.

Juneau

Kodiak I.

Sitka

CANADA

MONGOLIA

Aleutian Islands

Kuril Is.

UNITED
STATES

JAPAN

PACIFIC OCEAN

San Francisco

Los Angeles

CHINA

Hawaiian Islands

0   600 Miles

0   900 Kilometers

Czar Peter the Great was curious as to what lay beyond Russia's Siberian possessions. He was the first czar to send an expedition to find out whether Siberia and North America were linked.

tory of European contact with Alaska began in the reign of that most energetic of Russian czars, Peter the Great.

According to legend, Peter (czar from 1682 to 1725) was embarrassed during his European travels when geographers asked him about the extent of his Siberian possessions. Some mapmakers said that Siberia and North America were connected. Others said they were not. Peter simply didn't know. In fact, Peter's curiosity must have been fired by more than impertinent questions from geographers. The Russians had been moving steadily eastward across Siberia for more than a century. It was only a matter of time before they would come to the end of the land and wonder what was on the other side of the water. Peter was also aware that the British and Dutch were already searching for a Northwest Passage from the Atlantic to the Pacific, and that if the Russians could find such a passage from the Pacific side it would be a great triumph and possibly lead to the domination of a new and important trade route.

Shortly before his death in 1725, the czar commissioned Vitus Bering, a Dane who served with the Russian navy, to conduct an expedition. Part of the instructions Peter issued to Bering were:

> *You are to proceed . . . along the coast which extends to the north and which seems, in all probability (since we do not know where it ends), to be part of America.*

> *With this in view you are to try to find where it is joined to America, and to reach some city in European possession, and to inquire what it is called and to make note of it, and to secure exact information and to mark this on a map and then return home.*

The task sounded simple, but it was, in fact, enormous. A small army of men, including shipbuilders, had to be sent 5,000 miles (8,000 kilometers) from St. Petersburg to the Pacific coast of Siberia. For most of the route there were no roads, and the weather was simply horrible. It wasn't until July 1728 that Bering's newly constructed ship, christened the *St. Gabriel*, was finally launched.

Bering and his crew of forty-four men and officers sailed cautiously northward into the fog-shrouded sea. He passed through—and named—the Bering Strait, and convinced himself—correctly, as it turned out—that Asia and America were not joined. He came very close to the North American mainland, but because of the fog was unable to see it.

Bering returned to St. Petersburg to make his report. Though he was criticized in some quarters for having been too timid and for not really proving that Asia and North America were separate, Bering's accomplishments had been considerable. A second and more ambitious expedition was planned. It was called the Great Northern Expedition.

In the summer of 1741, Bering launched the *St. Peter* under his command, and the *St. Paul* commanded by Alexei Chirikov, from the east coast of Siberia's Kamchatka peninsula. Their task was to make a voyage to America and, if possible, to open trade between the two continents. From the start the expedition was shadowed by disasters.

One disaster was the result of a mapmaker's error. At that time maps customarily showed a large land mass in the North Pacific called Jeso or Gama Land. The land was entirely mythical, but Bering went in search of it. By the time he decided that no such place existed, precious days of the short northern summer had been wasted.

In the incessant fog and foul weather, the two ships of the expedition lost contact with one another. Both sailed eastward and both reached North America sometime around mid-July 1741. Chirikov's *St. Paul* was the first to make a landfall. He sent his mate and ten armed sailors ashore in a longboat in search of fresh water. They did not return and a search party found nothing. The

Extinct

AMONG THE CREATURES FIRST described by Georg Steller was an enormous relative of the manatee. It has been called Steller's sea cow. It grew to a length of up to 24 feet (7 meters) and weighed up to four tons. The sea cow was a gentle, slow-moving giant that was easy prey, even for the poorly equipped and half-starved members of Bering's ill-fated expedition. Steller described the flesh as tasting like "excellent beef." He thought that there were enormous numbers of these animals in the northern waters and that they would provide an abundant supply of meat for those who were to occupy the region. He had greatly overestimated the number of giant sea cows, and greatly underestimated the extent of the slaughter that was shortly to take place. Within thirty years of its discovery, this animal had been hunted to extinction. The only real record that we have of its existence are Steller's original descriptions, and this is his greatest claim to fame. Steller also described a large flightless cormorant—another prime target for hunters. It was extinct in a little more than a century. The destruction of Steller's sea cow was the first recorded extinction of a species of mammal in modern times. It was a grim omen of what was to come.

These three Steller's sea cows were drawn by a member of Bering's expedition. Since this animal has been extinct for more than 200 years, it can be remembered only through drawings.

following day the *St. Paul* was approached by two native boats. At that point Chirikov and his officers concluded that the landing party had probably been killed.

Time and supplies were running out and the crew of the *St. Paul* was ravaged by scurvy, a disease caused by a deficiency of vitamin C. Scurvy was common among sailors of that time because their diet did not include enough fruits and vegetables. Chirikov and his officers decided that they had fulfilled their mission and turned around and sailed back home. They reached Avacha Bay, on the Kamchatka peninsula in Siberia, the place from which they had departed, on October 8. During the five-month voyage, twenty-one of the eighty men of the *St. Paul* had been lost.

Bering's *St. Peter* was forced to endure far greater hardships. Battered almost constantly by gales, the *St. Peter*'s return was much slower. But one member of the crew was angry about returning at all. He was Georg Wilhelm Steller, a young German who was the resident scientist on Bering's expedition. He was the first scientist ever to observe the wonders of northwestern America. Steller urged Bering not to return, but to winter over in Alaska so he could study the land. The mariner, however, was old and ill, and like Chirikov he felt he had done what he had been sent to do. He wanted to go home.

At an island in the Gulf of Alaska, Steller joined a party that had been sent ashore for water, and he was allowed to spend a few hours gathering specimens. He bitterly complained. "We had come only for the purpose of bringing American water to Asia." Steller was an ill-tempered and quarrelsome young man with a colossal ego. He had a strong opinion about everything, and he was often right. But he was so widely disliked that he was rarely listened to.

After a dreadful return voyage during which many of the crew died of scurvy and Bering himself became desperately ill from the disease, the *St. Peter* sighted what they thought was the shore of Kamchatka, and on November 6, they landed. Unfortunately it was not Kamchatka at all, but a small island off the coast. The ship was so badly battered that the crew could not take it out again, and the men were so debilitated by disease that they could not build another ship. They were forced to spend the winter on the island. Bering and many others did not survive. But the robust Georg Steller did, and it gave him a chance to make the first careful observations of life of the region. He did not waste his opportunity.

2

"Soft Gold"

Among the animals encountered by the survivors of Bering's Great Northern Expedition during that terrible winter was the sea otter. The sea otter was not an unknown animal. It was found along the coast of Kamchatka and all the way down the Pacific coast of America. The natives of Kamchatka hunted the sea otter for its fur, but its pelt was not prized as highly as that of foxes and sables. The Spanish who occupied California had no need for or interest in sea otter furs.

The Russians were different. The *St. Peter*'s crew had hunted sea otters for food. Sea otters were fairly easy to catch and Steller had called them "the mildest of sea animals." The stranded Russians disliked the taste and texture of otter flesh, but facing starvation, they didn't have much choice. And they used otter pelts to keep warm. When the spring came and they were able to construct a new vessel with which to sail home, they stuffed the craft with as many otter pelts as it could hold.

When the *promyshlenniki,* the name given to the Russians who conducted most of the fur trade in Siberia, saw these glossy, five-foot-long (150-centimeter) skins, their eyes practically lighted up with joy and greed. They knew that these furs would command enormous prices in the Chinese fur market. They were so valuable they were called "soft gold." Few otter pelts were available in Siberia, and the *promyshlenniki* wanted more. They had already decimated the sable population of Siberia and they were looking for a new source of income. Suddenly this ragged band of mariners turned up with bundles of the precious otter pelts and tales that sea otters could be found in abundance in the newly explored lands.

Immediately the region fired the interest of not only geographers and scientists but also of entrepreneurs who envisioned fabulous wealth from the fur trade. If it had not been for the sea otter and its beautiful fur, the Russians would have been in no hurry to follow up on Bering's discoveries. Within a few years the hunt for fur led to the enslavement of the native Alaskans called Aleuts, and to the virtual extinction of the sea otter in that part of the world.

The *promyshlenniki* were trappers, not mariners. They knew nothing of shipbuilding and seafaring. But that did not stop them. They set out for Alaska in little ships made of green lumber lashed together with leather thongs and fitted with sails made of reindeer skins. Many of these makeshift vessels capsized or broke up in heavy seas. But the Russians kept on coming.

By 1745, the *promyshlenniki* were established on Attu Island at the western end of the Aleutians, the chain of islands stretching out from the Alaskan coast. They began encountering the Aleuts who lived on the island chain, who at the time may have been the most numerous of all the native Alaskan peoples. Alaska is an Aleut word meaning "mainland."

The Russians may have been no more brutal than the Spanish

were in their conquest of South and Central America or than the Americans were in their push westward across the continent. But it is a terrible story none the less. The *promyshlenniki,* who had been mistreating the Siberian natives for a century, regarded the Aleuts as barely human. As a general rule the Aleut men were slaughtered without provocation and the women and girls were enslaved. The Aleuts had no weapons to match the Russian muskets, and on their barren islands there were few places to hide. The Russians named Attu's harbor Massacre Bay.

In 1762, the Aleuts attempted to strike back at their oppressors and actually succeeded in killing some Russians and driving others back to their boats. But as word of the counterattack spread among the hunters, a man named Ivan Solovief managed to organize the generally rowdy and undisciplined *promyshlenniki* and began a reign of terror up and down the island chain. Over the next four years as many as 3,000 Aleuts (including men, women, and children) were slaughtered. Since there may have been as few as 10,000 Aleuts at the time, and probably no more than 25,000, this was a crushing blow. By the time Solovief's reign of terror was over, the Aleuts were a broken people, no longer free to live their own lives and rapidly declining in numbers.

At some point the Russians decided that it was not a good idea to kill all the Aleut men. It was much more profitable to put them to work hunting sea otters, a task at which they were far superior to the Russians. This, however, left the Aleuts little time to hunt fish and gather roots in the traditional way, and so they constantly faced starvation.

News of the atrocities filtered back to St. Petersburg, where the government regularly issued warnings against mistreating the natives. But thousands of miles away the *promyshlenniki* paid no attention. On the distant Aleutian Islands there was no government, no law of any kind, just the will (or perhaps the whim) of the greedy and brutal fur traders.

The *promyshlenniki* made no attempt to set up any sort of permanent settlement on the Aleutians or elsewhere in Alaska. They

The Aleuts were native to the chain of islands now known as the Aleutians, and were nearly enslaved by the promyshlenniki. *Their neighbors the Eskimos, or Inuit, inhabited Kodiak Island and fared much better with their Russian neighbors.*

built no trading posts—not even a single house. They lived in the same rude structures that the Aleuts lived in, and fathered many children who were later called Creoles by the Americans.

The first man to try and bring all of these activities under a single authority was a merchant named Grigory Ivanovich Shelekhov. In 1784 he led a well-equipped and well-financed expedition to set up a permanent colony. He brought his wife Natalia along, and she was the first—and for a long time the only—white woman to live in Alaska.

Shelekhov built a little village at a place called Three Saints Bay on Kodiak Island. The inhabitants of Kodiak were an Eskimo group called the Koniag with whom Shelekhov apparently was able to establish fairly good relations. He killed no one, and seems to have paid the Koniag adequately for the work they did.

In 1786, the Shelekhovs returned to St. Petersburg to begin a long and frustrating attempt to have the government give them an imperial charter that would allow them to establish a fur-trading monopoly in Alaska. The Court of Catherine the Great (empress of Russia from 1762 to 1796) was busy with wars and other matters, and the request was sidetracked. Shelekhov tried all sorts of stratagems to get the charter he wanted, including the offer to send missionaries to Kodiak Island at his own expense in order to enlist the Russian Orthodox Church on his side. But nothing worked.

In the meantime, Shelekhov's colony was going downhill because of poor management. He hired a new man to manage the colony: Alexander Baranov, a former glassmaker and Siberian fur trader. Though short, balding, and quite ordinary looking, Baranov was a man of enormous energy, intelligence, and imagination. By the time he died in 1819 he was to earn himself the unofficial title "Lord of Alaska."

Alexander Baranov, "Lord of Alaska" and its first appointed Russian governor.

Baranov organized—some said enslaved—the Aleuts to hunt sea otters. No matter how badly Baranov may have treated the Aleuts they were better off than when subjected to the random savagery of the *promyshlenniki*. Baranov fought a running battle with other Russian fur hunters, whom he considered poachers. He quarreled incessantly with the officers of the occasional Russian ship or those of other nationalities that visited his domain and with the missionaries of the Russian Orthodox Church. Baranov thought the missionaries were meddlesome and they thought he was godless. But slowly Baranov extended his power and influence.

The Aleuts were so efficient at hunting sea otters that the population of the animals was declining. Baranov had to expand the territory under his influence in order to keep the supply of pelts coming. In 1799 he led an expedition south down the coast of lower Alaska. Here, on a large wooded island that was later named after him, he built a small settlement and a fort. He named it St. Michael.

It was in this area that Baranov encountered a Native American people called the Tlingit. Unlike the Aleuts and Eskimos, who lived in regions so barren that their entire existence was consumed in the struggle for survival, the Tlingit lived in an area well supplied with food, timber, and other necessities. They had developed one of the most advanced native cultures in the Western Hemisphere. Among other accomplishments, they were masters of woodcarving, and Tlingit wooden masks and totem poles are regarded as among the great artistic creations of the world.

Comparatively numerous and well organized, the Tlingit were fierce warriors. One of their strongholds, called Sitka, was just a few miles south of where St. Michael was built. At first the Tlingit did not seem to resent the Russian intrusion, and Baranov confidently returned to Kodiak Island, leaving a colony of about 450 people behind. Then, in June 1802, the Tlingit attacked St. Michael, killing all the men they could get their hands on and carrying off the women as slaves. Some of the survivors were picked up by a British ship. They were taken back to Kodiak Island but held until Baranov paid a substantial ransom for their release.

This was the first news that Baranov had received of the attack. He burned for revenge, but he didn't have the weapons or the manpower to launch an immediate counterattack. However, outside events came together to give him what he needed. He had made a deal with an American sea captain. Baranov lent the American a force of Aleut hunters, who would catch sea otters along the California coast. The American would then split the profits with Baranov and give him some weapons, too. The weapons were relics of the American Revolution, but they were better than anything Baranov had.

Back in St. Petersburg, the fur monopoly charter that Shelekhov had first sought from Catherine the Great was finally granted. By that time both Shelekhov and Catherine were dead, but Czar Alexander I, who reigned from 1801 to 1825, gave the Russian-American Company, now headed by Shelekhov's son-in-law, Count Nikolay Rezanov, the right to control all Russian activities in Alaska. Baranov was officially appointed governor, though the title didn't add anything to his powers.

In the spring of 1804, Baranov—leading a force of *promyshlenniki* and Aleuts and armed with his American weapons—set out for Sitka. When he arrived he found a Russian warship already on the scene. Even then the battle for Sitka was not a foregone conclusion. The Tlingit nearly threw back the attackers, but finally gave way in the face of prolonged shelling from the ships.

Baranov built a new fort, which he called New Archangel but is known to history by its old name, Sitka.

In 1805, Baranov transferred his headquarters from Kodiak to Sitka. This marked the start of the brief but spectacular flowering of Russian America.

3

The Aristocrats of Sitka

Very quickly Sitka was transformed from an isolated frontier fur-trading outpost to a truly important Pacific port. Ships from many nations, particularly from the United States, made Sitka a regular stop. The traders would come from as far away as Boston. They would bring food, always a problem for Russia's Alaska outposts, and rum—a product popular with the Russians and disastrous for the native peoples. They traded for the Alaskan pelts and then sailed on to China, where they traded the furs for silk, tea, and other merchandise that fetched high prices in Europe and on the East Coast of America.

The basis of the Russian enterprise was still the fur of the sea otter. Most of those who ran the Russian enterprise had no thought of conservation. The sea otter was a resource to be exploited to its fullest. And when the supply of sea otters was depleted in one area, new hunting grounds had to be found. Grigory Shelekov, who had originally conceived the entire enterprise, put it this way: "For rapidly extending the power of the Russian people it is possible to step farther and farther along the shore on the American continent, at the furthest extension to California."

*Sitka, the Alaskan port that became a symbol of the elegance
and refinement of the Russian elite even in this remote territory.*

Count Nikolay Rezanov, whose attempts at establishing a Russian agricultural colony in Northern California resulted in both romance and tragedy.

His deputy, Alexander Baranov, had similar ambitions. So did his son-in-law and successor, Count Nikolay Rezanov. In 1805, Count Rezanov made a tour of his company's American outposts. In Sitka he met Baranov for the first time. Though the Lord of Alaska was famous for his willfulness, bad temper, and crude habits, the cultured Rezanov described him as a "wonderful man!" The two men thought alike about expanding Russian power and influence in America. In fact, Baranov had already sent one of his agents south to scout the California coast. The information the agent brought back was the subject of extended discussions between Rezanov and his governor. Baranov had even grander plans. He actually sent one of his agents to Hawaii, with the aim of extending Russian influence there. But the agent had the bad fortune to back the losing side in a civil war and had to run for his life. There were no further attempts to contact Hawaii, but California remained an object of interest.

The main problem for the Russians in America was a reliable supply of food. It was very expensive to send supplies from Siberia to Sitka. Yankee traders could provide the needed supplies at a much lower price, and Baranov had established excellent relations with American seamen. But the Russians felt that there were dangers in becoming too dependent on the Americans. Both Rezanov and Baranov realized that growing American power on the Pacific coast would pose a significant long-term threat to Russian interests in the region.

Another possible source of supplies for Russian America was the Spanish colonies in California. The Spanish were too weak and too disinterested to become a threat to Russian domination of the fur trade. But they were also forbidden, by royal decree, from trading with foreigners.

A third alternative was to establish a Russian agricultural colony in Northern California, the plan favored by both Rezanov and Baranov.

In 1806, Rezanov visited the Spanish port at San Francisco. This visit had consequences that were both romantic and tragic. It was said that the forty-two-year-old Russian count, who had been a widower for two years, fell in love with the sixteen-year-old daughter of the Spanish port commander. Though there was a great difference in age, the Russian nobleman was still handsome, intelligent, and rich—in short, quite a catch. But there was a problem. She was Catholic, he was Russian Orthodox. As a nobleman, he would need special permission to marry a Roman Catholic.

According to the story, he was hurrying back to St. Petersburg to obtain permission when he fell into an icy Siberian stream and caught pneumonia. Instead of taking the careful course and waiting until he recovered his strength, the impatient nobleman pushed on. A couple of days later he was so badly weakened that he fell from his horse, was kicked in the head, and died. The story continues that it was years before the Spanish girl waiting in San Francisco learned of the Russian's fate. Then she was so heartbroken that she refused to marry and spent the rest of her life doing charitable works.

Whatever the truth of the story, Count Rezanov's untimely death was a serious blow to Russian activities in America. Baranov was already sixty years old and was worn down by fifteen years of living under the brutal and primitive conditions of Alaska. He had told Rezanov that he wanted to be replaced. The request alarmed the count, who regarded his governor as indispensable. He persuaded Baranov to stay on, at least for a while. Now, with the count's death, Baranov had no choice but to stay.

Rezanov's death was a loss for another reason. He was the first of the Europeans or Americans to fully recognize that the supply of animals in Alaska was not inexhaustible. He knew that Steller's sea cow had already been hunted to extinction. He was also aware that sea otters were becoming harder and harder to find throughout their entire range.

When he visited the seal breeding grounds on the Pribilof Islands he was shocked by what he found. More than a million seals had already been killed for their fur. If the slaughter went on much longer there would be no seals left at all. The usual practice was to continue the hunt until there was nothing left and then to move on. But. Rezanov banned any further killing of seals on the Pribilofs until the population recovered. He was not soft-hearted about seals. He was simply farsighted enough to realize that some measure of conservation would be necessary if the fur trade was to continue into the future.

After Rezanov's death Russia's entire Alaskan enterprise was once again left in the hands of the aging Baranov. The old man had not lost any of his enthusiasm for establishing a Russian colony in California. But it wasn't until 1812 that he was able to follow through on his scheme. In March of that year he sent a force of 26 Russians and 102 Aleuts, led by his trusted associate Ivan Kuskov, to a spot some 65 miles (105 kilometers) north of San Francisco. There they constructed a fortified settlement. It was named Fort Ross, after an old form of the word *Rossiia*, or Russia. The plan was for the Russians to raise crops and animals that could then be shipped north to Sitka or other parts of Russian America. The primary task of the Aleuts was to hunt sea otters as they had done elsewhere.

The Spanish looked upon this sudden intrusion from the north with great suspicion. They became even more suspicious the following year when the Russians established another settlement just 25 miles (40 kilometers) north of San Francisco. Suspicious or not, there was really nothing that the Spanish could do. Spain's hold on its American colonies was weak and getting weaker.

The Spanish need not have worried, because Fort Ross was in trouble from the start. The area around the settlement was poor farmland, and the Russians themselves were very poor farmers.

The Aleuts were also supposed to help raise the cattle, but this was a task for which they were totally unsuited. The Aleut people had never raised cattle. They had never even seen cattle. These fearless sea hunters were frightened by cows. Instead of producing enough food to feed Russian Alaska, the Fort Ross colony was barely able to feed itself.

But Baranov continued to hope that the California colony would ultimately become a success. However, success (or failure) was something for the future. Baranov knew that he was getting much too old and feeble for the rigors and responsibilities of governing Russian America. He repeatedly petitioned St. Petersburg to be relieved of his duties. When his superiors finally did get around to sending a successor, there was a string of misfortunes. One of the appointees became sick and died on the way. Another was shipwrecked and drowned. It wasn't until 1817 that a living successor finally arrived at Sitka, and Baranov himself, now seventy-two, retired in 1818.

The old man elected to return to St. Petersburg by sea. This meant sailing three quarters of the way around the world, but it avoided the hardships of an overland journey across Siberia. While sailing through the tropics, the Lord of Alaska contracted a fever and died in April 1819. He was buried at sea, far from both his home and the land he had ruled almost as a king.

Baranov had basically been a fur trader, not so very different from the rough *promyshlenniki* that he governed. His successors were naval officers, often from the nobility. They brought their families, and at great expense, everything from fine wines to fine art to help relieve the monotony of life at the isolated outpost of Sitka.

Yankee whalers, who became increasingly frequent visitors to the seas around Alaska, told stories of the elegance and refinement of the Russian elite at Sitka. The stories sounded almost unbelievable, for this was such a remote part of the world. But the stories were true.

Baranov's successors were, by and large, a hardworking and responsible group of men who even made some serious attempts to improve the living conditions of the Aleuts and Indians and of the Russian workers who were often treated little better than the native Alaskans.

But Russian America had been built on "soft gold"—the fur of the sea otter—and through overhunting, the sea otter population was shrinking to the point of extinction. So despite its outward elegance, Sitka—and the whole of Russian America—was in serious economic decline. Its days were numbered.

4

The Decline of Russian America

Of the Russian-American Company governors who followed Baranov, the most energetic was Baron Ferdinand Petrovich von Wrangel. He was a thirty-four-year-old Arctic explorer and naval officer when he came to Sitka in 1830. By that time the sentiment for a strong Russian presence in America was on the wane in St. Petersburg. For the first time there was talk of giving up the American colonies entirely because they were no longer profitable.

Wrangel would hear none of that. Like Rezanov and Baranov before him, Wrangel was convinced that Russia had a great future in America if the colony was properly managed. He encouraged exploration of the interior of Alaska. In 1833, he sent an expedition north to map the coast, investigate the Yukon River delta, and build a post in the area. He also made significant studies of the lives of Alaska's native people.

The baron's boldest move was to put into place the first comprehensive conservation program on the North American continent. He restricted the hunting of fur seals to young males. In an attempt to preserve the falling sea otter population, Wrangel divided the whole Alaskan coast into strictly regulated hunting districts. Each district was closed to hunters every other year. Because of his policy, the sea otter began to make a comeback from the brink of extinction. Even so, the number of sea otter pelts shipped by the Russian-American Company had fallen by two thirds. Nothing could restore the huge profits that had been brought in during the Baranov years.

This painting, done in 1872, shows a large group of Alaskan fur seal pups. The farsighted conservation efforts of Baron Ferdinand Petrovich von Wrangel ensured that the widely hunted seal and sea otter would not meet extinction.

Wrangel's Russian-American Company also had to fight off advances by the Hudson's Bay Company. This British-based company, which was very similar to the Russian-American Company, had the fur-trading rights to British-controlled Canada. The Hudson's Bay Company began expanding its activities into the Russian area and Wrangel responded by building a fort to repel them. The British withdrew, but a few years later, by diplomatic negotiations, the Hudson's Bay Company was able to establish a foothold within the Russian boundaries.

Wrangel knew that the profits of the Russian-American Company had been declining and that the entire Alaskan enterprise was in jeopardy. There were two reasons for the fall in profitability. First was the enormous expense of providing food and other supplies for Alaska. Second was overhunting, which was reducing the sea otter population so drastically. The solution to both of these problems, Wrangel thought, could be found in revitalizing Fort Ross and expanding Russian colonies in California. This would provide cheaper food and greater access to California's large sea otter population.

Fort Ross had been a disappointment for the Russians almost from the start. But the political situation had changed since the colony was first established in 1812. In 1821, Mexico had won its independence from Spain. But Mexico still suffered from internal conflicts and faced the threat of foreign invasion. While Wrangel was governor of Alaska, he had been given tentative approval by the government of Czar Nicholas I (who reigned from 1825 to 1855) in St. Petersburg for a California expansion plan. Wrangel completed his term as governor in 1835, but he was still a director of the Russian-American Company. In 1836, the baron traveled to Mexico City to try and negotiate with Mexican president Santa Anna for more land in California.

When Wrangel arrived, Texas had just declared its independence from Mexico and defeated Santa Anna's efforts to put down the rebellion. This may not have been a good time for a foreigner like Wrangel to ask the Mexicans to give up other parts of their northern provinces. One thing that Santa Anna demanded was that Russia recognize his new republic as a legitimate state.

Wrangel believed that recognizing the Mexican republic was a good idea. He said that Mexico would appreciate the good will and realize that the settlement of a few Russians in the northern Mexican territories would present no threat to Mexico. In fact, he said, such settlements might help to block expansion by England and, especially, the United States.

Czar Nicholas saw matters differently. He didn't want to antagonize the English any further. The English were already alarmed by what they saw as the expansion of Russian power elsewhere in the world. Even more significantly, the czar did not want to support the Mexican government, which he viewed as revolutionary. Nicholas believed that the authority of monarchs must be maintained everywhere under all circumstances. The Mexicans had overthrown the authority of the king of Spain. Nicholas hoped that one day Spain would be able to reassert its authority over its former colony. Wrangel simply could not get the czar and other officials in St. Petersburg to share his vision of Russian domination of the North Pacific. So in the end the California expansion scheme came to nothing.

A few additional Russian outposts in California would probably have made no ultimate difference to Russian America. But the collapse of Wrangel's mission really marked the beginning of the end for the Russian enterprise. Instead of expanding its influence, Russia began to pull out of America. The first area to go was Fort Ross itself. It had never become self-sufficient, and the amount of money that the Russian-American Company had to pump into the colony just to keep it going grew from year to year.

By 1841, the Russians felt that they could no longer bear the expense of the California colony. They sold Fort Ross for $30,000 to a Swiss-American named John Sutter. Ironically, a few years later at another Sutter property, Sutter's Mill, just 120 miles (193 kilometers) east of Fort Ross, gold was discovered. It was this discovery that set off the famous California gold rush of 1849.

St. Petersburg, which was 10,000 difficult miles (16,000 kilometers) away from California, could never have controlled the turbulent gold rush. But the Russians did try to make some profit from it. When the gold rush began, the governor of Sitka virtually stripped the warehouses bare to supply the boomtown of San Francisco. A few years later Sitka developed a new industry, supplying ice to California coastal towns. During the 1850s, Alaska shipped more than 20,000 tons of sawdust-packed ice, at $35 a ton, to cool the drinks of Californians.

These enterprises could not replace the depleted fur trade. And so the Russian empire began looking around for ways to sell its unprofitable American territory.

In 1854 there was a bizarre scheme to turn Alaska over to the San Francisco company that imported Alaskan ice. Russia was just about to go to war with England, and officials of the Russian-American Company believed that their government was too weak and distracted to protect Alaska. They reasoned that the British would not dare touch American property. The Americans simply wanted to protect their source of supply. The contract specified that after a few years the ice company would return Alaska to the Russians.

The plan was really a fraud. Edouard de Stoeckl, the Russian minister in Washington, rejected it. So did the American government. The British insisted that they had absolutely no interest in Alaska. The British signed an agreement with the Russians that they would leave Alaska alone if Russia agreed not to invade Canada.

Two years later, after the war with England ended in a shattering and expensive defeat for Russia, negotiations for the sale of Alaska began once again, this time in earnest.

The Voyage of the Shenandoah

ONE OF THE STRANGEST EPI-SODES of the American Civil War was played out in Alaskan and Siberian waters. In 1864, Confederate agents in England secretly purchased a warship they christened the *Shenandoah*. The ship could operate under both sail and steam, and was reported to be the fastest ship afloat. It carried eight guns, six of them powerful sixty-eight pounders. Its mission was to sail to the North Pacific to disrupt the American whaling fleet, which the Confederates said was "a source of abundant wealth to our enemies and a nursery for their seamen." That the Confederates would use their limited resources to try to destroy the North Pacific whaling fleet is an indication of just how important and profitable whaling had become.

By the following year, the swift and well-armed Confederate raider was creating havoc among the Yankee whalers. During its voyage, the *Shenandoah* either destroyed or ransomed thirty-eight ships, took 1,053 prisoners, and did damage totaling $1,361,983. America's North Pacific whaling fleet was nearly destroyed in a single season.

There wasn't a ship in the vicinity that could challenge the *Shenandoah*, but the northern weather was not to be tamed by speed or guns. As colder weather began to close in and ice floes appeared, the *Shenandoah* crunched into a field of ice. The crew managed with difficulty to get the craft out of the ice, but that was enough of the frigid climate for them. They headed south toward the California coast.

The Confederate ship Shenandoah *towing prisoners during the Civil War. This ship was a major contributor to the decline of whaling in North America.*

They planned to steam into San Francisco harbor and lay siege to the city. By the time they arrived the war was over and the Confederacy was at an end.

After a great deal of diplomatic wrangling the British agreed to pay compensation, but the whaling fleet never really recovered. The real winners of this part of the Civil War may have been the whales of the North. They continued to be hunted for decades after 1865, but the hunting fleet had diminished considerably.

5

The Americans Take Over

When the Russians began a serious campaign to sell their American territories, they found an eager buyer in America's exuberant secretary of state, William H. Seward. Seward was an energetic and ambitious man who yearned to be president, though he never really became a serious challenger. He certainly typified the expansionist mood of mid-nineteenth-century America. Seward didn't want just Alaska; he envisioned the United States taking over Hawaii and the Philippines, and to the north Greenland, Iceland, and even Canada.

The sale resulted in lots of criticism. Alaska was dubbed "Seward's Icebox" and more frequently "Seward's Folly." Alaska was portrayed as a frozen and worthless wasteland. One humorist suggested that the territory should be named "Walrussia." Some opposition newspapers said that the purchase had been made solely to divert public attention from the problems of President Andrew Johnson's administration. The Johnson administration did have serious problems, and the year after the Alaska Purchase President Johnson was very nearly impeached. There were also warnings that the bold American move into the North Pacific would provoke the British.

James Gordon Bennett, the flamboyant editor of the *New York Herald*, ridiculed the sale by running a mock advertisement telling any European sovereign who wished to unload worthless land to contact Seward. In fact, Bennett was in favor of the Alaska Purchase; he just wanted to ridicule the politicians a bit.

When the treaty signed by Seward and Stoeckl came up for ratification in the Senate, Charles Sumner of Massachusetts spoke out strongly for it. He painted a picture of vast potential wealth from "forests of pine and fir waiting for the axe; then the mineral

Secretary of State William H. Seward was both ridiculed and praised for his purchase of Alaska, which some called "Seward's Icebox."

products, among which are coal and copper, if not iron, silver, lead, and gold." Senator Sumner acknowledged that the two greatest Alaskan industries were the fur trade and fishing—"fisheries which, in waters superabundant with animal life beyond any of the globe, seem to promise a new commerce." But even the Massachusetts senator could not resist a little dig at the treaty by noting that Alaska also contained, "the two great products of New England, granite and ice."

The average American may have had only a vague idea of where Alaska was, or what it might be used for, but he or she probably felt it was a good thing to acquire such a huge territory for such a modest price. However, the purchase of Alaska was not a subject that commanded a great deal of attention from the public. The government hadn't given it much thought either. No one was sure what was to be done with this vast new land.

The formal ceremony that turned over the Russian territories in America to the United States was held in Sitka on October 18, 1867. It was a poorly attended embarrassment. The American and Russian military were on hand. A few hopeful businessmen and a reporter or two from San Francisco were there. Some curious Russians, Indians, and Creoles looked on—but that was about all. As the Russian flag was lowered to be replaced by the Stars and Stripes, it got stuck and a Russian sailor had to be hoisted up the pole in order to cut it down. That was too much for Princess Maria Maksutov, wife of Prince Dimitri Maksutov, the last governor of Russian America. She and her husband had bitterly opposed the sale of Alaska. At this final indignity, she burst into tears.

A newspaper correspondent from San Francisco produced a glowing, if inaccurate, account of the event. "Democratic institutions now extend over an area hitherto the possession of a despotic

The signing of the Alaska Purchase Treaty, shown here, took place in March 1867, but the formal ceremony in which the territory was turned over was held seven months later in Sitka, and was poorly attended.

government. The occasion inspired the soul of every American present and as the officers retired three mighty cheers were given and we all rejoiced that we now stood on American soil."

Several hundred Russian employees of the Russian-American Company had, under the treaty, been given the option of returning to Russia or staying in Alaska and becoming American citizens.

[47]

Brigadier General Lovell Rousseau, who formally received Alaska for the United States, predicted that the Russians would stay "if kindly treated." But the Russians were abused by undisciplined American troops and within weeks almost all returned home. The promise of "democratic institutions" held no allure for them. A departing Russian officer described the Americans as "riff-raff." The Creoles, who were of mixed Russian, Eskimo, Aleut or Indian ancestry, stayed—they had no place else to go.

With the departure of the Russians there were about 30,000 indigenous peoples, who lived in isolated places throughout the vast territory. There were about 900 Americans, almost all of them concentrated in Sitka.

The Alaska Purchase had been carried out so rapidly and with so little planning that the territory's legal status was unknown. The transfer of the land took place before the bill appropriating funds for payment was ratified. That didn't happen until July 1868.

So at first Alaska was neither a state nor a territory. There wasn't a single copy of the U.S. Constitution to be found anywhere in Alaska. Alaskans couldn't legally incorporate a town, buy or sell land, or even impanel a jury for a trial.

The Americans in Alaska did not let legal niceties stand in their way. They went ahead and framed a city charter for Sitka and elected a mayor, five councilmen, a recorder, a surveyor, and a marshal. They levied their own taxes, made their own laws, and meted out their own punishments to lawbreakers. It was very much rough-and-ready "frontier justice."

When Congress finally got around to appropriating the money for the purchase of Alaska, they also got around to trying to decide what sort of government it should have. During the debate on the appropriation, Representative Hiram Price of Iowa said: "Now that we have got it [Alaska] and cannot give it away or lose it, I hope we will keep it under military rule and get along with as little expense as possible."

And that's just what happened. Congress established a military district and a U.S. customs district, which extended the laws of customs, commerce, and navigation to Alaska. The officer put in charge of the military district had an improbable name, Major General Jefferson C. Davis, the same name as the president of the recently defeated Confederate States of America. The administration of the Military District of Alaska was left pretty much up to the whims of General Davis. He was an easygoing soul who seemed to let his increasingly rowdy troops do whatever they wished.

Liquor was banned in the military district, but the soldiers managed to replace a mild Native American beverage made up of bark and berries with one made from molasses and yeast, distilled into an eye-popping concoction called *hoochinoo*. This beverage was so notorious that a shortened form of the word—*hooch*—soon took its place in American slang as a synonym for raw liquor.

The American takeover of Alaska was off to a bad start.

6

Stumbling into the Future

In August 1869, Secretary of State William H. Seward traveled to Sitka to reassure the increasingly unhappy Americans that the political future for them would be bright. He said, "the political society to be constructed here, first as a territory, and ultimately as a state or many states, will prove a worthy constituency of the Republic." Ultimately Seward was right. But it would be ninety years before Alaska finally became a state in 1959. In the meantime, things were going from bad to worse.

In 1873, Sitka's city council simply ceased to exist. Its last meeting was held on February 18. There is no indication in the minutes of this meeting that the council had decided to dissolve. It just didn't meet again. William S. Dodge, the city's first mayor and the first customs collector for Alaska, had given up both jobs in frustration and gone back to California. The city's second mayor, John Kinkead, lasted less than a year before he, too, became disillusioned and sailed south. The problems of governing Alaska were overwhelming and there was no support or guidance coming from Washington.

Many of those who had come north in the hopes of making a quick fortune or of finding a new and more prosperous way of life found only bitter cold and hardship. They quickly gave up on their dreams and headed back where they had come from.

The once elegant Russian colonial capital was sliding into bankruptcy and near anarchy. The board sidewalks, which were the only protection against the summer mud, went unrepaired. There were no facilities for waste removal, and filth was everywhere.

The only bright spot—if it can be called that—was on the Pribilof Islands. In 1870, Congress passed an act making the islands a federal reserve. When the Russians pulled out, seal hunting on the Pribilofs became unregulated and extinction from overhunting again threatened the animals. Congressional action strictly limited seal hunting. This was done more to please the wealthy West Coast investors, who had bought all the assets of the now defunct Russian-American Company and leased the Pribilofs from the government, than from a concern for seals. The investors wanted to protect their investment from extinction and to ward off competition from other seal hunters. The seals were nearly exterminated anyway.

Aside from this single act, no other substantial Alaskan legislation was passed until 1884. As far as Congress was concerned, Alaska practically didn't exist. Remember that for much of the nineteenth century a trip from Washington to Alaska could take weeks or even months. And during the winter months you couldn't get there at all. Alaska was just too far away and too cold to be of much real interest.

In 1877, the troops in Alaska were pulled out to help deal with an uprising among the Nez Perces in Idaho and Montana. Now the only U.S. officials left in all of Alaska were Montgomery P. Berry, the customs collector at Sitka; three postmasters; and a few treasury agents in the Pribilofs. To police the 586,400-square-mile

(944,100-square-kilometer) territory, Berry had two cases of rifles and two cases of ammunition that had been shipped to him by mistake. No one, aside from Berry himself, was even authorized to use the rifles.

Among his other duties, Berry had to enforce the prohibition against liquor smuggling in the vast territory. The army had never been able to enforce the prohibition and now the customs collector, without even a single rowboat at his command, was supposed to patrol 34,000 miles (54,700 kilometers) of ragged and remote coastline and countless islands. It was obviously an impossible task, and while both Americans and native Alaskans may have been short of many provisions, they were never short of liquor.

The Alaskans had complained bitterly about the inefficient and often corrupt army rule. But now, with the soldiers gone, they felt totally unprotected. Conflicts between the small white population of Alaska and the native Alaskans (particularly the Tlingit, who had never reconciled themselves to white rule) flared up regularly. These conflicts were often fueled by alcohol. In 1878, a gang of drunken whites was accused of setting fire to an Indian woman's cabin and burning her alive. As a result of incidents like this, violent street fights broke out in Sitka in 1879. Some Sitka residents, fearing an Indian revolt, sent an urgent plea to Washington. But not trusting in their government's ability to help them, they also sent a plea to British Columbia in Canada.

The first help to arrive was Her Majesty's warship *Osprey*, which steamed into Sitka's harbor on March 1, 1879. The captain of the *Osprey* turned his guns on the Tlingit village outside of Sitka and announced that the ship would stay until the United States government did something about protecting its own citizens. The following day a small U.S. revenue cutter arrived, but the *Osprey* remained at Sitka for over a month until the U.S.S. *Alaska* arrived on April 30. In June the *Alaska* was replaced by the *Jamestown*. The whole incident was an acute embarrassment for the U.S. government.

After the arrival of the *Jamestown*, the navy assumed effective control of Alaska. That was not a position the navy wanted or was really fit for. The *Jamestown*'s commander, Lester A. Beardslee, complained that "acts be performed by us which could not be justified by any law except the natural law by which might becomes right."

When Beardslee's successor, Commander Henry Glass, asked the secretary of the navy what he was supposed to do with three civilians who were charged with attempted murder, the secretary replied that since there were no courts he should just keep the men in confinement as long as he thought necessary.

As much as Washington may have wished to ignore Alaska, there were other forces at work that made this policy of neglect harder to stick to. One of these forces was an energetic Presbyterian missionary named Dr. Sheldon Jackson. Jackson was not only a missionary to Alaska; he became a missionary *for* Alaska. He spent part of the year in Alaska and the rest traveling around the United States preaching to Christian groups about the territory in which there was no law and no restraint: "and the lowest animal passions of the rough miners, trappers, hunters, soldiers, and sailors rage unchecked. The Indian woman is considered the lawful spoil of these men!"

Jackson was a powerful and persuasive speaker who mobilized Christian opinion toward the goal of bringing law and order to Alaska. Jackson moved on to Washington, where he lobbied powerfully for appropriations to Alaskan schools. More than any other single individual of his day, Jackson made the people of the United States conscious of the responsibilities they had to the vast land purchased in that hectic meeting on March 30, 1867.

An even more powerful influence on public opinion toward Alaska was the discovery of gold. The first gold prospectors began drifting into Alaska in the 1870s. Most had come up from the gold fields of California, which were already being depleted. The first major gold strike occurred on Alaska's southeastern coast in 1880. The discoverers were a pair of drunken prospectors, Joseph Juneau and Richard Harris, who literally stumbled across the find. As news of the find leaked out, other prospectors rushed to the area, and a few became fabulously wealthy. Neither Juneau nor Harris ever made a great deal from their discovery and both died penniless. A town, which later grew to a city and became the capital of Alaska, was built near the site of the discovery and named in honor of Joseph Juneau.

Gold was never the principal source of Alaska's wealth. But gold has a way of capturing the human imagination like nothing else. It brought Alaska to the attention of the world. And the discovery even made Washington realize that it could no longer continue to ignore "Seward's Icebox." On May 17, 1884, Congress passed what was called the Organic Act of Alaska. The act placed Alaska under the civil and criminal laws of Oregon. There was also to be a governor appointed by the president of the United States. There were other provisions in the act, including one that held that Alaskan natives were not to be disturbed in the possession of any lands actually in their use or occupation or claimed by them. The final disposition of any native claims was to be settled by future congressional action.

There was much about the Organic act that was sketchy and makeshift. For example, it did not provide for any Alaskan legisla-

The town of Juneau, named after one of the prospectors who discovered gold in Alaska, went from this humble beginning to become the capital of the state.

Although gold never became a major source of wealth for Alaska, its allure brought many adventurous types to the territory. Prospectors braved all kinds of weather in pursuit of gold.

ture. Also, there could be no jury trials in Alaska, because jurors had to be selected from among taxpayers and there were no provisions in the law for levying taxes. But for all its shortcomings, the act did, for the first time, provide Alaskans with a basic government structure.

In 1884 Alaska was still a long way from Seward's promise of eventual statehood—but the process had finally begun.

Many factors influenced Alaska's development, but two stand out—war and oil.

During World War II the Japanese threatened the coast of Alaska, and this spurred a military buildup. The Alaska Highway, which did so much to open up the territory, was built in 1942, primarily for military purposes.

After World War II, the United States immediately plunged into the era known as the Cold War. It was a forty-year confrontation between the United States and Russia—or the Soviet Union, as it was then called. Alaska, just across the Bering Strait from the Soviet Union, had great military significance. Throughout the Cold War the military buildup in Alaska continued.

Some oil had been discovered in Alaska in the 1950s, shortly before Alaska became a state. The discovery helped push the territory toward statehood in 1959. But these early discoveries were nothing compared to the vast deposits of oil and natural gas that were discovered in the Arctic coastal plain, or North Slope, in 1968. Commercial oil production from these fields began in 1977 when a pipeline was built across the Alaskan tundra.

As a result of the North Slope discoveries, there was something of a population boom in Alaska. But today Alaska, despite being the largest of the states, remains one of the least populated. It still deserves the title of the "Last Frontier."

Chronology

Perhaps 10,000 to 12,000 years ago	First humans cross from Siberia to Alaska
Seventeenth century	First European mariners sight Alaska
1728	Vitus Bering sets off on first voyage to America (July)
1741	Second Bering voyage, the Great Northern Expedition, sets sail for America in summer. Bering's ship is wrecked November 6; survivors forced to spend the winter on a small island
1745	Russian fur traders established in Aleutian Islands
1784	Merchant Grigory Shelekhov sets up colony on Kodiak Island
1786	Alexander Baranov hired to manage Alaskan colony
1799	Baranov establishes colony at St. Michael
1802	Tlingit attack St. Michael (June)
1804	Charter granted to Russian-American Company; Baranov attacks Tlingit at Sitka

1805	Baranov moves his headquarters from Kodiak to Sitka; Count Nikolay Rezanov tours Russia's American possessions
1812	Russia establishes Ft. Ross in California (March)
1818	Baranov retires
1830	Baron Ferdinand Petrovich von Wrangel becomes governor of Alaska
1841	Russians sell Ft. Ross to John Sutter
1856	Russia defeated in Crimean War
1867	Alaska Purchase treaty signed March 30; Russia's American territory officially turned over to the United States at Sitka ceremony, October 18
1868	Congress ratifies appropriation bill for funding Alaska Purchase (June)
1870	Pribilof Islands become a federal reserve, leased to a private commercial company
1877	Army leaves Alaska
1879	British ship arrives at Sitka to protect Americans (March 1)
1880	First major gold find in Alaska
1884	Congress passes Organic Act of Alaska (May 17)

Further Reading

Cobb, Vicki. *This Place Is Cold*. New York: Walker, 1990.

Hunt, William R. *Alaska, A Bicentennial History*. New York: Norton, 1976.

Ragan, John D. *The Explorers of Alaska*. New York: Chelsea House, 1992.

Wheeler, Keith. *The Alaskans*. Alexandria, VA: Time-Life Books, 1977.

Younkin, Paula. *Indians of the Arctic and Subarctic*. New York: Facts on File, 1991.

Bibliography

Bancroft, Hubert. *Alaska*. New York: Antiquarian, reprint 1960.

Chevingny, Hector. *The Lord of Alaska*. New York: Viking, 1942.

Hinckley, Theodore C. *The Americanization of Alaska*. Palo Alto, California: Pacific Books, 1972.

Hunt, William R. *Arctic Passage*. New York: Scribner's, 1975.

Jensen, Ronald J. *The Alaska Purchase and Russian-American Relations*. Seattle: University of Washington Press, 1975.

Naske, Claus M. *Alaska: A History of the 49th State*. Norman: University of Oklahoma Press, 1994.

Okus, S. B. *The Russian-American Company*. Cambridge, Massachusetts: Harvard University Press, 1951.

Pierce, Richard A. *Builders of Alaska*. Anchorage: Limestone Press, 1985.

Tompkins, Stuart R. *Alaska: Promyshlennik and Sourdoughs*. Norman: University of Oklahoma Press, 1945.

Index